THE WILTON HOUSE 'RIDING SCHOOL'

Introduced by

Dorian Williams

 Harvey Miller Publishers

The Wilton House 'Riding School'

Introduction

THE PARTICULAR charm of this unique and delightful set of pictures is that they are by an enthusiastic, dedicated and, it would seem, expert horseman who was also an equally enthusiastic and talented but amateur artist.

Baron Reis d'Eisenberg lived in the middle of the eighteenth century and was a horseman whose ability was renowned throughout Europe. The book, 'Description du MANEGE MODERNE', of which these pictures were a part, was widely read, firmly establishing the Baron's reputation as a horseman of renown. From such evidence as is available it would appear that for most of his adult life he was attached as an Ecuyer, or Riding Master, to the Court of the Hapsburgs, first under Charles VI and later under Francis I. There are frequent references in the 'cartouches' beneath each picture to the Emperors. One (no. 39) depicts the horse on which Charles VI was mounted at his Coronation. It is of interest to recall that it was under Charles VI that the famous Spanish Riding School in Vienna, designed by the eminent Fischer von Erlach, was completed in 1735.

1. **Spanish horse: bright bay in colour, called Coracon**
2. **Chestnut barbe from Tunis** *Overleaf.*
As explained in the text, horses from many countries were used for haute-école, but there is little doubt that the Spanish and Arab breeds were the most popular. The exact description of the Spanish horse's coat in no. 1 is shiny: in other words, has a sheen on it.

In another 'cartouche' (no. 8) it is stated that the horse belonged to the Prince de Schwartzenberg, Grand Ecuyer de l'Empereur Charles VI, which suggests that Reis d'Eisenberg succeeded him as Grand Ecuyer. After the death of Charles VI it would appear, from constant reference in the 'cartouches' to the horses of Francis I, husband of Charles' successor Marie Thérèse, that the Baron continued to serve the Imperial Household. It is worth noting that many of the horses depicted come from countries that were part of the Hapsburg Empire—Hungary, Moravia, Silesia, Bohemia.

There is no doubt, however, that the fame of Reis d'Eisenberg extended beyond the bounds of the Empire: nor, from all that the pictures suggest, that he was widely travelled, either in attendance on the Emperor or on his own. It is likely that he spent many years in Italy where he could bring his knowledge of and enthusiasm for haute-école to the various Principalities. For it was at this time that throughout Europe there was the revival of interest in high-school riding. It was a 'craze' amongst the aristocracy such as, at a different period, real tennis, or the composition of music for the dance, or the writing and performing of plays.

For the latter some delightful little theatres were built: for haute-école some magnificent riding halls were constructed, the most famous of all being the Spanish Riding School in Vienna, which d'Eisenberg may well have visited himself. As an English horse is depicted in one of his pictures (no. 5) and as it is known that one edition of his book was dedicated to King George II of England, it is likely that he also visited England; there one of his friends and acquaintances was the 10th Earl of Pembroke whose name is amongst those of the

British nobility who subscribed to the edition.

The author was also the artist; thus we have this unique comment on the newly discovered art of haute-école: unique in that the illustrator is as great an expert as the author, being one and the same person.

While the conformation of his horses may leave something to be desired compared with a Stubbs or a Ferneley, his knowledge of classical riding ensures that the high-school movements depicted are absolutely correct. The pictures are enhanced enormously by the delicate, romantic backgrounds against which the horses are placed, the colour invariably showing off the central figure to great advantage.

But it is the depicting of the whole range of the classical movements that is of primary interest. It would be very satisfying if there had been a constant progression in classical riding since Xenophon wrote his famous treatise in 400 BC: but this is far from true. The principles of Xenophon were widely accepted over that part of the world dominated by the Greeks, but as a result of wars, the fall of the Greek empire and a shift of emphasis in human priorities, the art of classical riding was completely lost for over 2000 years. Fortunately the precepts and principles of Xenophon, based, in fact, on an even earlier equitation authority, Simon of Athens, are adhered to today by all the great riding masters of the world. In a few words it can be said that Xenophon based his training, firstly on intuition, a complete understanding between horse and rider: secondly, on kindness. As he so aptly put it, and remarkably

remembering that it was written nearly 2500 years ago, 'Nothing forced or not properly understood can ever be beautiful'. Simon of Athens apparently went even further. Xenophon quoted him as comparing the high-school horse with a dance. 'A dancer forced to dance by whip and spur would be no more beautiful than a horse similarly trained'.

The Simon of Athens book has been lost but, fortunately after the disappearance of so many of the cultural arts, Xenophon's own book survived and it was on this that the renaissance of classical riding was based at the beginning of the seventeenth century. It is not easy exactly to say how this came about, but in the world of culture gradually, at the end of many centuries of darkness, there was a glimmer of light. It is established almost beyond doubt that it was Naples that first saw the dawn in classical riding. A certain Frederico Grisone had studied Xenophon's book in great depth and, quoting lavishly, produced his own book on high-school equitation. Where he differed was in his insistence on a greater use of force. Grisone's most outstanding pupil was Pignatelli who became Ecuyer at the famous Riding Academy at Naples.

One of Pignatelli's pupils was the youthful Pluvinel who came to Naples from France and was later to become Court Riding Master to Louis XIII of France. His own book, Manège de Roi, broadly based on Pignatelli's methods which were in turn, based on Grisone's, which, in their turn, were based on Xenophon's and Simon's, nevertheless advocated more humane methods, discarding the use of force, thus returning to the principle held in Greece 2000 years earlier. Though at first Pluvinel's precepts were widely ridiculed, gradually they became accepted, and were adopted by François

de la Guerinière, perhaps the greatest seventeenth century riding master. In contrast the Duke of Newcastle in his famous and elaborate book produced in 1657 advocated much more forceful, even cruel methods of training: and, therefore, proved unacceptable. De la Guerinière held the field unrivalled and during the next century had enormous influence, even the Spanish Riding School basing its training on his methods.

With the French Revolution much was lost, but fortunately Vienna survived. Thanks to Max Ritter von Weyrother, head of the school at the beginning of the nineteenth century, the influence of Vienna spread far and wide: an influence so strong that even the great master Baucher in France could make little headway: Fillis in England even less, which resulted in his going to Petrograd. Right up to the outbreak of the first world war it was the Spanish Riding School, now under Gebhart, that exerted the greatest influence in Europe in the field of haute-école. Between the wars at Saumur the Cadre Noir did much to re-establish the influence that France had wielded at the time of de la Guerinière: but after the second world war it was once again the Spanish Riding School of Vienna with their famous Lippizaners under Colonel Alois Podhajsky that completely dominated the classical scene. It was my father, Colonel V. D. S. Williams, a great friend of Podhajsky, who was responsible, in the thirties, for introducing high-school riding into Britain.

Thus over 300 years most of the great European nations, Italy, France, Austria, Germany, England have played a part in the development of haute-école. The value of this set of pictures is that they are the product of a man who was not only an artist but also a recognised authority in the greatest heyday of haute-école.

What exactly is haute-école, high-school riding? Somewhat to over-simplify one could say that the nearest analogy is the relationship of ballet to ballroom dancing. One can indulge in the latter with little more than a sense of rhythm and an ability to learn simple steps. To be a ballet dancer one has to go through rigorous training because demands are made on the body and limbs that are never required in ballroom dancing: the more advanced the standard, the more rigorous the training. So with equitation: a natural balance and the ability to learn simple 'aids' is enough to enable the ordinary person to ride adequately and to train his horse to go through the paces, walk, trot, canter, even to jump, in such a way as to give pleasure in safety. In fact, 'dressage' means little more than this: simple, basic training. To extend the ability of a horse to carry out more complicated movements—a simple example, to do an extended trot as well as a controlled trot—demands more exacting training on the part of the rider to enable him to train the horse. To train a horse to Olympic Grand Prix standard, which includes such movements as the Pirouette, Passage and Piaffe, demands exceptional skill. But a horse can be trained even

3. German bred horse from the stud of Comte de Salippe
The German bred horse, whose colour is described as Porcelain piebald, but as we would say, dapple, was given to the Duke of Lorraine and Bar, later Emperor, who sent him to the Riding Academy at Luneville where he was schooled by the Baron d'Eisenberg. Known as Superb, he was the admiration of the whole world, especially with his piaffe, the last word in perfection.

further, as in Vienna, to do the famous airs, or exercises above the ground—passade, levade, courbette, croupade, capriole, which obviously demand exceptional expertise.

Anyone can go for a trot on a horse: to train a horse to do the capriole is very exceptional. In the same way anyone can do a fox-trot: only the most talented dancer can achieve 22 fouettés. Baron d'Eisenberg's pictures illustrate the complete range of high-school movements, from the simplest to the most complex, as will be seen.

Is a special horse needed for haute-école? It is quite clear from the picture that at least in the eighteenth century horses from many countries were considered suitable, including the English (no. 12). It is interesting, too, to observe the different types of horses used as models for the pictures. The Arab, the Thoroughbred, the chunky English horse, the powerful, compact Andalusian: and all colours, including skewbalds. Gradually during the present century, especially in latter years, there has been an increasing tendency to regard the strong, solid Germanic type of horse as ideal for dressage, especially advanced dressage, and high-school: horses bred in Germany, Sweden, Holland. It seems to be the mode now, in the highest dressage circles, to consider the breeds with more quality less suitable. Whether this is really so, or whether it is a passing fashion is not easy to determine. Without doubt the emphasis today is very much on accuracy, each step and movement having to be exact: great discipline is exerted: there is the minimum of freedom, rather a complete control. For this the temperament of the Germanic type of horse is considered ideal, while the more volatile breeds do not find it easy to accept such control and discipline.

Yet as recently as the 1968 Mexico Olympics the medals went to the most attractive, light-footed, light-on-the-hand Russians, as different from the heavy Germanic breeds as it is possible to imagine. It is not so long since the French with strong Arab influence in their horses dominated the scene. Opinion is divided: today the Germanic dominates, though the apparent leaning towards greater quality in the Lippizaners at Vienna suggests that the pendulum may swing again. One cannot help feeling that the Baron, used to seeing every type of animal from every country, all employed in haute-école and all depicted in his paintings, would have been a little sceptical. Haute-école, one feels he would have remarked, is something that any aristocrat would be expected to practise, with any horse in his stable: whether it be Barb, Turk, German, Italian, Spanish, Danish, Arab, even English.

4. *Right above.* **Black Neapolitan bred from the stud of Count Conversano**
5. *Right below.* **English Bred horse: not the most beautiful**
The prefix Conversano is still found at the Spanish Riding School of Vienna: one of the most famous lines in high school breeding. The Baron appears to have had no very high opinion of English horses and notes that this one is speckled on its near side.

6. *Overleaf left.* **Turkish bred horse**
7. *Overleaf right.* **An Arab, bay brown in colour, from Morocco**
Baron d'Eisenberg attached great importance to colour. The Turkish horse is described as having a coat like a silver trout, the Arab as being coffee-brown in colour and particularly supple behind the saddle. Apparently the Baron rode a horse similar to the Arab for several months in London for a friend, achieving great success with it.

8
The correct seat for a classical horseman
The straightness of the leg is of extraordinary interest. This is the
complete exaggeration of the dressage seat, the near straight leg
position being used until late in the eighteenth century: when
riders started jumping fences the stirrup leathers were shortened:
but only in England.

Basic movements
Nos. 8-15

THE BASIC movements for the horse are the walk, the trot, the canter, which extend to the gallop. But there is also the halt or the stationary position. This, in fact, is of great importance as it is not natural for a horse to stand still for any length of time. Being originally a herd animal the horse tends when on its own to roam, looking for the rest of the herd: when with other horses to follow them. A horse, therefore, has to be trained to stand still. When stationary he should be 'four square': that is to say that he should have a leg at each corner (as depicted in nos. 8 and 9): one foot should not be in front of the other; nor should the horse be taking the weight off one of his legs. In dressage competitions the judges are strict on horses having the proper stance.

Surprisingly, perhaps, the walk is the least natural of a horse's gaits. Loose in a field he tends to jog or trot, unless he is grazing. The correct walk is level, well-balanced, relaxed. The sound of the footsteps should be like a metronome one, two, three, four: absolutely level, strongly rhythmic. At the walk, too, the horse should be absolutely straight. The head should be steady, properly 'on the bit', as it is said, which means that the head is not carried too low making a heavy contact on the hand, or carried too high 'above the bit', in which case it is difficult for the rider properly to control the horse, even at the walk.

There are in dressage three kinds of trots, the medium, which is really the normal, the collected and the extended. The normal trot which, like the

walk, should be steady, straight and controlled is ridden with the rider rising. At the collected trot the rider remains seated in the saddle with a firmer control of the horse. Both trots are two-time in which each diagonal pair of legs (near front and off-hind, and vice-versa) touch the ground together. The speed at the ordinary trot is approximately 200 yards a minute: the collected trot slightly stronger and therefore usually a little faster.

At the extended trot the horse stretches itself fully, pushing its forelegs well out in front but at the same time bringing its hind legs well underneath it. The extended trot is one of the most effective and dramatic movements in haute-école.

As with the walk it is essential in the trot that the horse's head should be carried level and steady with the rider maintaining a contact that is neither too heavy nor too light. The horse should never be allowed to nod up and down: ideally, too, the tail, should not swish from side to side, or revolve, which denotes a certain resistance whereas correctly there should be an impression of relaxed harmony.

There is a further trot, the most complex of all and very much a high-school movement rather than a natural gait: this is the passage; but we shall consider this later.

9
Correct use of the Cavesson
Again we see the straight leg. We can also see the boot reaching above the knee up the thigh. When riders started jumping, the top of the boot was folded over, showing the unpolished leather: hence the 'top-boot'.

10

Colt in action

In these two pictures we can see the difference between the
cavesson, a head-piece, used for training the young horse, and
the bit. The cavesson has a heavy nose-band, but no bit. Today it
is used only for lungeing, but not as a bridle. The long-cheeked bit

11

Trained horse in action

in no. 11, a spotted horse reared at the Imperial Stud of Bohemia (note brand on flank), is a severe bit demanding very sympathetic contact. There seems to be some confusion between Tiger, as this horse is called, and leopard which is the animal normally associated with spots.

12

Grey English horse ambling

The horse in no. 12 is an attempt to depict a horse ambling. The amble was a pace, particularly used by travellers and originally the English 'packmen', which is something between a walk and a trot: it would be called a jog today. In no. 13 we see the amble again,

13
Amble on the haunches
but in this picture it is used in the un-natural 'on the haunches' movement, no longer practised, the hocks being lowered as for a pesade (see no. 40). The chestnut in no. 13 was from the Conversano stud.

14

The extended trot

The extended, or fast trot, is not as exaggerated as we know it today, but contrasts with the collected trot. No. 14 is being ridden on a cavesson and is called Isobel. It is possible that Isobel was the name for a colour. The horse appears to be roan with a white tail:

15
The collected trot
possibly similar to a palomino. The rider uses a single long cheeked curb for the collected trot. The horse called Mille Fleurs was bred at the Stud of the Grand Duke of Tuscany, who later became Emperor.

Basic exercises
Nos. 16-25

Among the most straightforward exercises are the 'shoulder-in', the 'passage', the 'turn on the haunches' and the 'pirouette'. Probably the first in which the horse is schooled is the 'shoulder-in', the first of the lateral exercises: this is to increase a horse's suppleness, get him used to the aids, in particular the use of the legs, and to make him obedient. By lateral is meant the ability of a horse to move not only forwards but at the same time sideways. Basically 'shoulder-in', to the left and to the right is an exercise rather than a performance. Exercises in this category include the 'travers'—quarters-in, head to the wall; 'renvers'—quarters out, tail to the wall; 'half-pass'—the horse going sideways and forwards; 'full-pass'—the horse going completely sideways.

In the 'passage' which is a highly spectacular movement the horse performs the trot, swinging forward from one pair of diagonals to the other, in the ordinary sequence, but suspending the pair of legs in the air for a markedly longer period than at the trot. Ideally the horse at the passage gives an impression of floating, almost as if suspended on wings. In classical riding the passage must be absolutely level. The passage that one sometimes sees performed by liberty horses at a circus as a

16
Shoulder-in to the left
17
Overleaf. **Shoulder-in to the right**
The shoulder-in is one of the early basic training movements in dressage. In no. 16 the rider uses only a cavesson. In no. 17 he uses a single rein on the curb. No. 16 is rather delightfully described as cherry bay: in other words, a bright red bay. No. 17 is bay brown, or dark bay.

rule lacks this levelness and rhythm because they have been trained too hurriedly. One could almost say that the correct passage gives the impression of a trot in slow motion.

Usually the passage is done on a straight line, following the walls of the school or manège, but it can also be done on a turn, either a turn of 180° before advancing or a full turn so that the movement becomes a pirouette at the passage (nos. 20-23).

Developed from the shoulder-in exercise we get the 'volte', which translated simply means 'turn'. As the horse describes the turn it is bent in the direction of the turn so that the head is always inclined in the direction that the turn is following. There can be either a full turn or a half turn.

It should be emphasised that apart from the passage these movements are purely a part of training. The more advanced movements, which are depicted later in the series and will be dealt with a little later, could never be performed unless a horse had received this basic training.

As always, in these exercises and movements the rider has to maintain a steady, rather than a loose or severe contact on the horse's mouth, the head always remaining steady and the whole body of the horse balanced.

17 Shoulder-in to the right

18
Passage against the wall

The passage as described in the text is an exaggerated high stepping trot. To teach a horse to do it with no movement forward or very little, as when marking time, the horse was trained against a wall

19.

19
Passage against a barrier
or barrier. No. 18 is attractively described as the colour of ermine.
no. 19 is described as Souvet, presumably jet black. In no. 18 the
rider uses the cavesson, in no. 19 a single rein.

20
Passage turning to the left
Again in no. 20 only a cavesson is used: in no. 21 a single rein.
Again in no. 20 we get the description of 'tiger' for a horse

21

Passage turning to the right

leopard like in its marking. The horse, which would appear to be
the same in both pictures, is of Danish blood.

22
Passage at full circle to right
Both the 'cherry bay' and the dapple grey are performing a move-
ment that is very nearly a pirouette, though in a pirouette the

23
Passage at full circle to left
hind feet remain stationary. This could be described as a circular
marking time.

24
Turn on the forehand to right

In the turn on the forehand the forelegs remain stationary while the hind legs revolve round them in a partial, half or full circle. This is an early exercise in dressage training. The grey in no. 24 is

25
Turn on the forehand to left
being ridden in a double bridle, depicted for the first time in these
pictures. A single rein is used in no. 25 on the black horse with
three white socks.

Basic exercises at the canter
Nos. 26-37

It is interesting that there is no word in French for canter. Paradoxically the indication is that horses on the Continent canter rather than gallop so the 'galop' in France becomes a canter. The reason for this stems from the fact that whereas in the seventeenth, eighteenth and nineteenth centuries the concentration in England was largely on moving at speed because of the hunting, so that at one time the English were known as the galloping nation, on the Continent, because of the terrain and because the interest in high-school riding was more developed, the concentration was on collected riding.

Despite the efforts of the Duke of Newcastle, referred to earlier, the manège and the riding hall were virtually unknown to England, whereas on the Continent they were a part of every court, every aristocratic household.

The gallop in French, therefore, refers to a very much more sedate pace than the ventre-à-terre pace frequently enjoyed in England, depicted in sporting prints of the time.

It would not be possible to carry out exercises and training movements at the gallop in England: it was no problem on the Continent. It was perfectly easy at a canter, which was probably a slower pace than the trot, to execute turns, even pirouettes and it was these that formed the basis of exercises at the 'galop'.

The canter is a three-time pace in which three hoof beats are heard in the following sequence; near hind, near fore and off hind together, off fore (leading leg): or off hind, off fore and near hind together, near fore (leading leg). A horse turning to the right will lead with the off fore, to the left with the near fore.

26. 'Gallop' leading with near fore
27. *Overleaf*. 'Gallop' leading with off fore

No. 26 is really a collected canter while no. 27 'à demi-hauche' implies a stilted canter with the hocks lowered. An extraordinary story is associated with the horse in no. 26. Trained by de Regenthal, Riding Master at the Austrian State School, it was killed in a Carousel rehearsal when the spear of its rider, Count de Lengheim, entered its right flank. He had leased the horse from de Regenthal paying a deposit of 1000 florins (about £10,000) which de Regenthal claimed. Baron d'Eisenberg was apparently present at the time.

De Regenthal also trained the Bohemian-bred horse in no. 27.

The extended canter or gallop is seen only in nos. 28 and 29, in the other pictures one sees turns being executed at a highly collected canter. It is natural for a horse to turn from the middle: that is to say moving both the fore and the hind legs, pivoting from the middle. In dressage there are two exercises; the turn on the forehand and the turn on the haunches. The former is a useful exercise, making the horse pivot round on his forelegs which remain stationary, the feet on the same spot: but in the opinion of some people it is an un-natural exercise. It is of interest, therefore, that in this series only the turn on the haunches is depicted (nos. 30 to 33). At the canter this in fact becomes a pirouette (nos. 34-37).

The horse, if observed carefully, will be seen to pivot on the inside hind leg, picking his feet up in the direction in which he is going. The hind feet describe a much smaller circle or, more accurately, half-circle while the fore-feet describe a large circle, the outside leg crossing over the inside leg. Having described a half-turn or a full-turn the horse then goes forward without losing his rhythm.

The pirouette (nos. 36 and 37) is one of the most effective movements in all haute-école: also one of the most difficult. As with the turn on the haunches the rhythm should be maintained and the whole should appear balanced and flowing rather than jerky. For a full pirouette a horse will employ some six or eight strides; three or four in the half piroue-ette. The inside hind leg provides the centre of the circle which the forehand then describes.

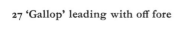

27 'Gallop' leading with off fore

28
Full gallop on loose rein
The pictures are probably intended to show horses at the extended
canter, first leading with the near fore, then with the off fore.
Because of the speed of the legs in action, artists always found it
difficult accurately to depict horses galloping until the invention

29
Full gallop, off fore leading

of photography. The horse in no. 28 was of Spanish origin, was
black with white socks and a wall eye. In no. 29 we have another
spotted horse again described as being like a tiger.

30
Half turn to the right
In no. 30 the horse is a skewbald. It is interesting and, one would
have thought, unusual to find these piebalds and skewbalds on
the Continent in the eighteenth century.

31
Half turn to the left
The horse in no. 31 is described as iron grey, a term commonly
used today. The rider in no. 30 rides on the cavesson, in no. 31 on
the bit, using a single rein.

32
Half turn to the left at the canter
These movements are carried out at a collected canter, though as explained in the text, the word 'gallop' was used for all three-time paces. The elegant dapple grey in no. 32 was from the de Kaunitz

33
Half turn to the right at the canter
Stud. The Spanish horse in no. 33 is described as burnt chestnut today we would say liver chestnut. The Stud brand carries the royal cipher.

34
Circle to the right
These close circles would appear to be performed in this same exaggerated movement with the hocks lowered. The nearest equivalent today is a very collected canter. The horse in no. 34, a 'golden' chestnut from the Dietrichstein Stud in Moravia, is being ridden in a double bridle while no. 35 is ridden on a single

35

Circle to the left

rein. The latter, trained by de Regenthal, one of the artist's
instructors, for the Emperor Joseph, was small but very supple
so that he could lower his hocks till his tail trailed on the ground.
The background of this picture is St. Mark's in Florence.

36
Pirouette to the right

In no 36 the pirouette is performed with the hind legs stationary, the fore legs carried close to the ground. In no. 37 the forelegs are higher. Charles VI brought the horse in no. 36 to Spain: it was trained by de Regenthal and was called Four White Socks. No. 37

37
Pirouette to the left
shows Prince Charles, brother of the Emperor, riding a roan horse called Peso d'Oro. He was trained by Baron d'Eisenberg for two and a half years at Luneville.

More advanced movements I
Nos. 38-45

THE PIAFFE, a very advanced movement, is included in top class dressage tests, but beyond that movements and exercises such as the pesade and the courbette are never included in competitions.

The piaffe could be described as a trot on the spot, or marking time. There is a moment of suspension as the horse steps from one diagonal pair of legs to the other. It is incorrect if the horse only lifts the diagonal legs when the others are already on the ground. The movement, when well

38. Piaffe to the left
39. *Overleaf.* Piaffe to the right

The piaffe, to the layman, is a horse marking time. The horse in no. 38 was Neapolitan bred and had clipped ears, a fashion that did not, mercifully, last long. The rider is none other than d'Eisenberg himself when he was Riding Master to the Count de Daun in Naples.

Charles VI rode the horse in no. 39 at his Coronation. De Regenthal, who trained him, called him superb as he surpassed all other horses, especially at the piaffe, being dead level which is the perfection in the piaffe.

done, should appear light and airy almost giving an impression of dancing. Throughout the movement the horse should remain strictly straight and on one spot, with no suggestion of the horse crossing his legs or swaying.

It is also possible to do a complete 360° turn at the piaffe (nos. 38 and 39) in which case it is more than ever essential that the horse remains balanced and steady, never losing the exact rhythm of his steps.

The pesade (nos. 40 and 41) was the original high-school movement, divorced from basic exercises, by Riding Masters in the eighteenth century. It consists of the horse lifting his forelegs off the ground, at the same time lowering his hocks, the body being maintained for several seconds at an angle of 45°. Nearly two hundred years later an extension of this movement was introduced known as the levade when the body was maintained at an angle of 30°, a position frequently seen in equestrian statues and now a part of the display of the Spanish Riding School of Vienna. If the pesade or levade is performed without the horse lowering his hocks then the horse is merely rearing.

The natural development from the pesade or levade is the courbette (nos. 42-45). This is when the horse maintaining his pesade position leaps forward in a series of steps on the hind legs. The courbette of today is somewhat different from that produced by the early Riding Masters, known as the mezair. In this movement the horse performed a series of short jumps, the head dipping almost to the ground between jumps, but little forward movement being achieved. At Vienna the cour-

bette is always at first performed in hand, that is with no rider on the horse's back. The number of jumps varies from two to five according to the ability of the horse.

The contact between the rider and the horse's mouth is of extreme importance as it will be appreciated that if the contact is too firm the horse could well be pulled over backwards. Attention is drawn to the importance of this by the fact that in two of the pictures (nos. 43 and 45) a cavesson (see caption to no. 9) is used, while in the other pictures a single rein is used (nos. 42 and 44).

It is of interest to note that nowadays in the performance of these movements by riders of the Spanish School the riders invariably ride without stirrups. To press down against the stirrups might result in the rider pulling against the horse with the increased purchase available.

39 Piaffe to the right

40
Pesade to the left

The pesade is a movement during which the horse squats on his haunches at an angle of approximately 45°. No. 40 shows an oddly

41
Pesade to the right
marked piebald in a magnificent riding hall, while no. 41 shows
a skewbald. In no. 40 the cavesson is used: in no. 41 a single rein.

42
Courbette to the left

As a rule this movement is maintained on a straight line, but it
would seem that there was a time when it was executed bearing to
the left or to the right. The dark brown in no. 42 was trained by
Baron d'Eisenberg himself, coming originally from the Feschen
Stud in Silesia. It was apparently possessed of a delightful temper-

43
Courbette to the right

ament and, therefore known as Agreeable, giving great pleasure to the rider. The Baron was also responsible for training no. 43 which is ridden in side-reins, selling him to the Marquess of Ligneville who took him to Sicily and sold him for 180 pistoles. The horse was a bright bay.

44
Advanced courbette to the right

These advanced courbettes are performed at a lower angle, 30°
as compared with 45° and, therefore, more difficult, putting a
greater strain on the haunches. The head is turned towards the
wall or barrier. The courbette was something quite new in

45
Advanced courbette to the left
training at this time. It was considered something near perfection.
Both horses are in side-reins. The rider in no. 45 was Count Joseph
de Par, considered to have outstanding talent.

More advanced movements II
Nos. 46-55

THE FIRST movements shown in these pictures are known as the schools above the ground and can only be performed by stallions possessing great physical strength: exceptional intelligence is also demanded. The pesade, the levade and the courbette can also be included in the schools above the ground as can the croupade, but they are less advanced than the capriole.

The croupade (nos. 46 and 47) could be described as a preparation for the courbette. The

46
Croupade between the pillars
47
47. *Overleaf.* **Croupade**
The pillars are still used at the Spanish Riding School of Vienna: usually they are for horses without a rider, but in no. 46 obviously assist the horse to perform a croupade without moving forward. In no. 47 only a cavesson is used. This horse was Polish, called Botte, belonging to the Prince Lubomirski who gave it to the Prince de Craon at Luneville.

horse leaps from the ground in a position similar to the courbette with his legs tucked underneath his body. The body is at an angle to the ground, not horizontal and not, therefore, a capriole.

Advancing from the croupade we have the ballotade (nos. 48 and 49) when the jump is higher with the hind legs turned back so that from behind one can see the horse's shoes. There is, however, no kick-back. Gradually as the horse jumps higher so his body will become more horizontal to the ground.

Finally of all the great schools or 'airs' above the ground we come to the capriole (nos. 50 and 51) the most testing and certainly the most theatrical of all the high-school movements. The stallion leaps simultaneously with all four feet off the ground: at the height of its leap with its body strictly horziontal to the ground, it kicks violently back with its hind legs. It is alleged that this derives from a medieval battle technique by means of which a knight could throw off his attackers: but not surprisingly this is in dispute.

After the dramatic energy of the capriole we are shown in these pictures first the rein back (nos. 52 and 53) and finally the halt (nos 54 and 55). In the rein back the horse should move both straight and steady. In fact in the rein back the horse employs the sequence of the trot, rather than that of the walk, lifting the diagonal feet off the ground and putting them down together.

In no. 54 we see a normal but exaggerated halt, the horse drawing its hocks underneath him, almost giving an impression of sitting down. In no. 55 the horse comes to a halt lifting its forelegs. This is an unusual movement no longer practised in high-school work.

It should, perhaps, be emphasised that haute-école was very much the prerogative of the aristocracy, as is suggested by the backgrounds in these pictures. In the seventeenth, and eighteenth centuries it was very much the fashion for a great aristocrat to have himself painted performing an haute-école movement, even if it is improbable that he was himself capable of such a performance, not having the time, possibly the inclination, to reach a high standard in classical riding. It was, of course, the great Riding Masters, mentioned earlier, who were the brilliant horsemen who developed riding to such an art. It would seem, then, that the Baron Reis d'Eisenberg was an exception, an aristocrat possessed of great riding ability which, of course, enabled him as an artist to depict accurately the complex movements of high-school.

For two thousand years the horse had been little more than a beast of burden. Suddenly in the seventeenth century it was elevated to a vital possession in man's search for artistic achievement. There is no doubt that the status of the horse today owes much to this. It is probably also true, however, that developing haute-école in the courts and palaces of Europe led to the erroneous assumption that riding was only for the wealthy. There was a great gap between those who practised haute-école in the great riding halls of their mansions and the peasants who used their horses on the land, or the soldiery who fought on them and used them to pull their guns, But if the contrast was more pronounced in equestrianism, contrasts in fact were evident in every facet of life. All forms of art have depended on enthusiastic patrons fortunately endowed with great wealth. Equestrian art is no exception.

47 Croupade

48
Ballotade to the left
Again these leaps forward were probably performed on a slight

49
Ballotade to the right

turn as well as straight forward. In no. 48 the piebald performs
with a single rein, while no. 49 is ridden on the cavesson.

50

The stop and jump

There is little difference between the movement described as stop
and jump and the capriole. In each the horse lashes out backwards.
when it is parallel to the ground in a strictly horizontal position
The horse in no. 50 called Curioso, another famous name in

51
Capriole

haute-école, was trained by de Regenthal and considered exceptionally able. The capriole done on one spot with no forward movement in no. 51 shows a horse of great lightness and elevation able to jump ten or twelve times, though he was not easy to train—by de Regenthal—and was, therefore, called Difficult.

52
Rein back on single rein

No. 52 belonged to the Duke Francis of Lorraine and Bar, later Emperor. It was trained by d'Eisenberg himself. No. 53 was a liver

53
Rein back on cavesson
chestnut with lighter points. The rein back must be both regular
in its rhythm and absolutely straight.

54
Halt on the haunches

In no. 54 we again see this exaggerated lowering of the hocks in certain movements. This Danish horse was called Tratrarat. The halt with the forelegs raised was considered by Baron d'Eisenberg

55
Halt en talcade

as one of the most beautiful and brilliant movements in haute-école. Apparently he used this movement with the full approval of the connoisseurs. A bright bay, the horse in the picture was Spanish.

Title page of "Description du MANEGE MODERNE" published in 1747. The text was written by Baron Reis d'Eisenberg, who also drew the illustrations which were engraved by B. Picart. The illustrations form the basis of the gouaches hanging in Wilton House and reproduced here. The backgrounds to these paintings do not appear in the engravings in the book.

© 1978, Harvey Miller,
20 Marryat Road, London SW19 5BD, England
Designed by Roger Davies
Printed by de Lange/van Leer . Deventer . Holland
Manufactured in Holland